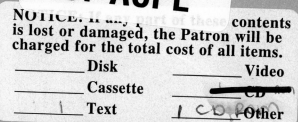

World of Dinosaurs

CHANHASSEN, MINNESOTA · LONDON

Two-Can Publishing
an imprint of Creative Publishing international, Inc.
18705 Lake Drive East
Chanhassen, MN 55317
1-800-328-3895
www.two-canpublishing.com

Created by
act-two
346 Old Street
London EC1V 9RB

Written by: Lucy Poddington
Edited by: Lisa Miles, Deborah Kespert
Story by: Mandy Ross
Consultants: Mike Benton (subject); Sandra Jenkins (educational)
Art director: Belinda Webster
Design: Rob and Maggi Howells, Liz Adcock
Main illustrations: Stephen Holmes
Computer illustrations: Jon Stuart
Line illustrations: Andy Hamilton

ISBN 1-58728-627-0

Library of Congress Cataloging-in-Publication data: pending

Photographic credits: p7: Corbis/Jim Zuckerman; p8: Corbis/Jonathan Blair;
p9: Ardea Ltd/Francois Gohier; p11: Oxford Scientific Films/Stan Osolinski; p16:
Ardea Ltd/Francois Gohier; p17: PA Photos/John Stillwell; p19: Ardea Ltd/Arthur Hayward;
p20: Oxford Scientific Films/E.R. Degginger/AA; p22: Oxford Scientific Films/Breck P. Kent;
p25: Ardea Ltd/Francois Gohier

1 2 3 4 5 6 08 07 06 05 04 03

Printed in Hong Kong

What's Inside?

This book is about dinosaurs, which lived thousands of years ago. There are no dinosaurs alive today. Sometimes dinosaurs' names are difficult to say. On your disk, you'll find a guide to help. Just print it out and use it together with your book.

What's on the Disk?

There are five great games to play on the disk. Just drive your car around the dinosaur park and visit the animals. Each one takes you to an exciting game. Catch up with the Tyrannosaurus for an extra surprise!

▶ Here's the screen that takes you to your games. Just drive up and visit each dinosaur.

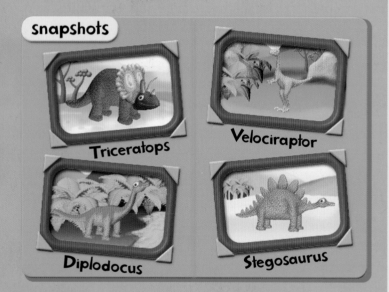

snapshots

Triceratops

Velociraptor

Diplodocus

Stegosaurus

picture album

Your Picture Album
When you play a game, you win a dinosaur photo for your picture album. There are four photos for you to collect. Try clicking on each one to see what happens.

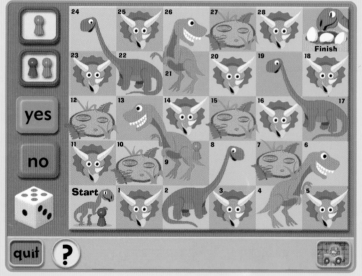

DISK LINK

Dinosaur Dash
Click on the Velociraptor to play a fantastic board game. Help the baby dinosaur race back to the nest by answering some questions. And watch out for the scary Tyrannosaurus!

DISK LINK

Bone Zone

Visit the Diplodocus to help the scientist build an enormous dinosaur. Answer each question and watch the bones drop into place.

DISK LINK

Spot It!

Go to the Triceratops to see the dinosaurs out and about. Can you spot each one? Watch what happens when you get your answers right.

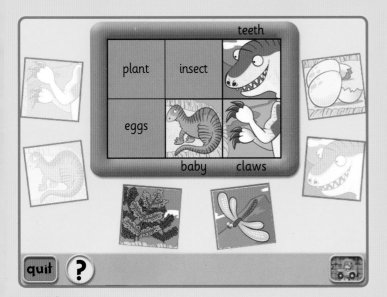

DISK LINK

Jigsaw Fun

Meet up with the Stegosaurus to make two fantastic dinosaur jigsaws. To play, match each word to its picture, then drag the pieces into place. There's a printout prize to color in, too!

DISK LINK

It's a Bonus!

After finishing two games, catch up with the Tyrannosaurus to play a bonus game. Guess which dinosaur is in the magnifying glass and win stickers to make a great dinosaur scene.

Diplodocus

Millions of years ago, the world was a warm, wet place. Tall trees, steamy swamps, and thick bushes covered the ground. Huge creatures called dinosaurs roamed the land. The Diplodocus shown here was one of the longest dinosaurs.

It's a fact!

Not all dinosaurs were enormous. A dinosaur called Compsognathus was about the size of a chicken.

Diplodocus had four sturdy legs to hold up its heavy body.

Diplodocus used its tail like a whip to swipe at its enemies.

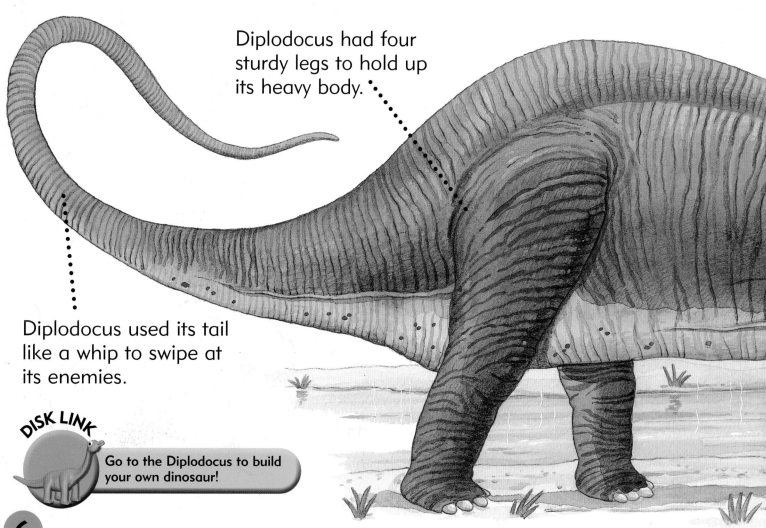

DISK LINK

Go to the Diplodocus to build your own dinosaur!

6

Diplodocus strolled with its long neck stretched out for a great view of its surroundings.

Biting juicy leaves from tall trees was a good way to eat on the move.

This is a model of Brachiosaurus. It was another long-necked giant. It could wade through swamps with its long legs.

Allosaurus

When fierce Allosaurus came charging through the trees, most other dinosaurs ran for their lives. Allosaurus liked to dine on gentle, plant-eating dinosaurs. It grabbed them with its claws and sunk in its teeth.

Allosaurus's huge head was a terrifying sight!

Allosaurus's roar probably sounded like a rumble of thunder.

Experts find out about dinosaurs by digging up bones. They piece the bones together just like a jigsaw puzzle.

It's a fact!

Allosaurus had an amazing mouth that opened really wide. This beast could snap up small dinosaurs whole!

Sharp, curved claws were useful for tearing into meat.

This is the skull of an Allosaurus. Its mouth was packed with more than 70 jagged teeth for tearing meat.

Allosaurus walked on two thick, powerful legs.

Stegosaurus

Stegosaurus spent most of the day munching leaves and twigs. When it wanted to nibble at taller bushes, it stood up on its long back legs. Special plates grew from Stegosaurus's body. These helped to scare away hungry meat eaters.

Stegosaurus had to eat lots of leaves to fill its large belly!

It's a fact!

The plates on Stegosaurus's back were so big that you could use one as a backrest!

DISK LINK

Go to the Stegosaurus to piece together a dino jigsaw puzzle.

3 1833 04024 309 6

10

Meat eaters such as Allosaurus ate Stegosaurus for dinner.

No one knows what color dinosaurs were. The maker of this Stegosaurus model gave it yellow stripes to help it to hide in the forest.

Two rows of tall plates grew along Stegosaurus's back and tail.

Attackers had to watch out for these sharp tail spikes.

Weird Creatures

When dinosaurs ruled the land, the sea was full of unusual reptiles and other strange creatures. Giant animals flew in the sky, on the lookout for a snack. Let's take a look at some of these amazing beasts!

Ophthalmosaurus's huge eyes helped it to spot tasty fish in the murky water.

Elasmosaurus hunted other sea animals. It stretched out its long neck to grab food.

Elasmosaurus used its strong flippers to paddle through the water.

Fierce Pterodactylus
soared in the air, flapping
its huge, leathery wings.

It's a fact!

When gigantic
Quetzalcoatlus
opened its wings
to fly, it was as
wide as a small
airplane!

This strange-looking
fish is a Coelacanth.
Coelacanths are still
living today!

Dinnertime!

Most of the dinosaurs are munching their leafy dinner. But watch out! Allosaurus is on the hunt for a meaty feast!

Allosaurus

Stegosaurus

Pterodactylus

Diplodocus

Words you know

Here are some words that you learned earlier. Say them out loud, then try to find the things in the picture.

tail	claws	spikes
head	neck	plates

Where does the tall Diplodocus find its food?

Tyrannosaurus

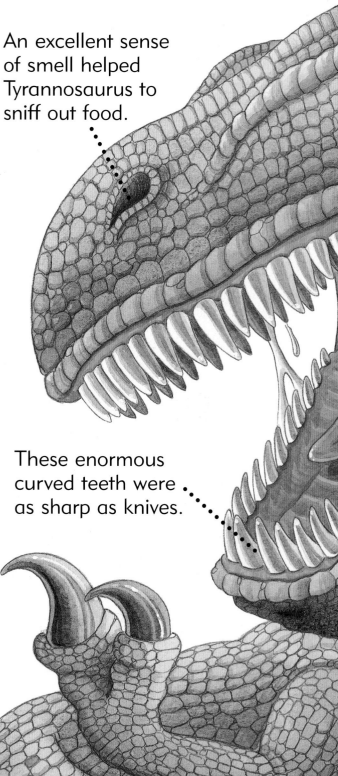

An excellent sense of smell helped Tyrannosaurus to sniff out food.

Mighty Tyrannosaurus was one of the scariest dinosaurs ever! It would sneak up on its dinner, then pounce. Other dinosaurs had no chance against the Tyrannosaurus's snapping teeth and deadly claws.

This tooth from a Tyrannosaurus is longer than an adult's hand! If it lost a tooth, it simply grew a new one.

These enormous curved teeth were as sharp as knives.

DISK LINK

Go to the Tyrannosaurus to spot the dinosaurs close up!

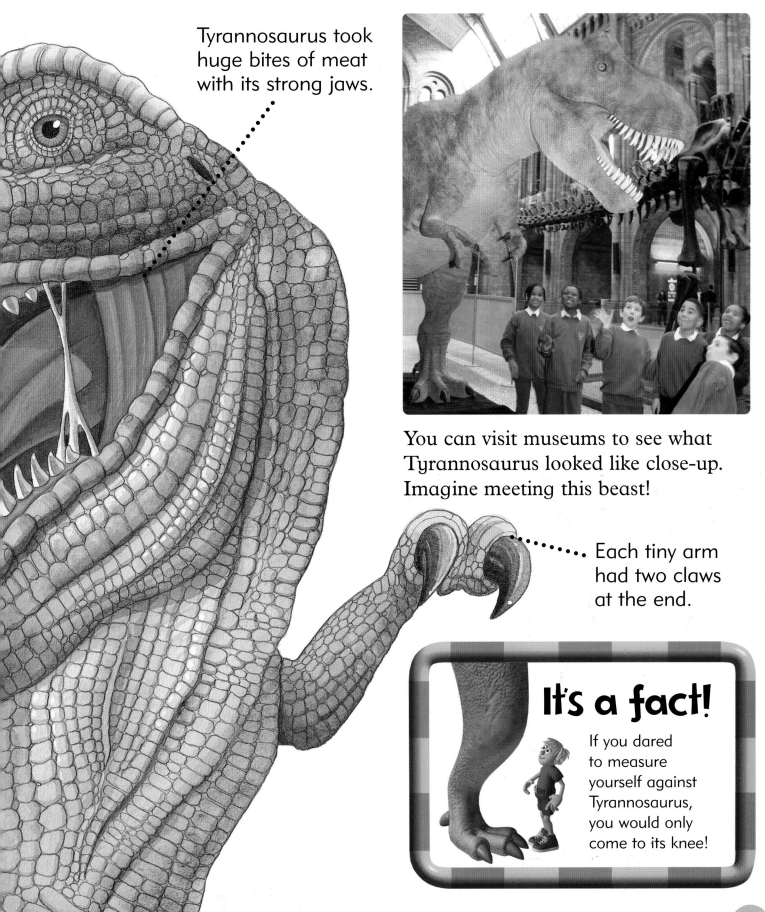

Tyrannosaurus took huge bites of meat with its strong jaws.

You can visit museums to see what Tyrannosaurus looked like close-up. Imagine meeting this beast!

Each tiny arm had two claws at the end.

It's a fact!

If you dared to measure yourself against Tyrannosaurus, you would only come to its knee!

Ankylosaurus

Ankylosaurus had a clever way of protecting itself. Tough skin and bony spikes covered all of its body except for its belly. No matter how hard they tried, most hungry enemies could not get past this suit of armor.

Thick, bumpy skin covered Ankylosaurus's large body.

A knobby club at the end of the tail sent enemies flying.

It's a fact!

One kind of armored ankylosaur even had a hard, bony belly. You could jump on it and not make a dent!

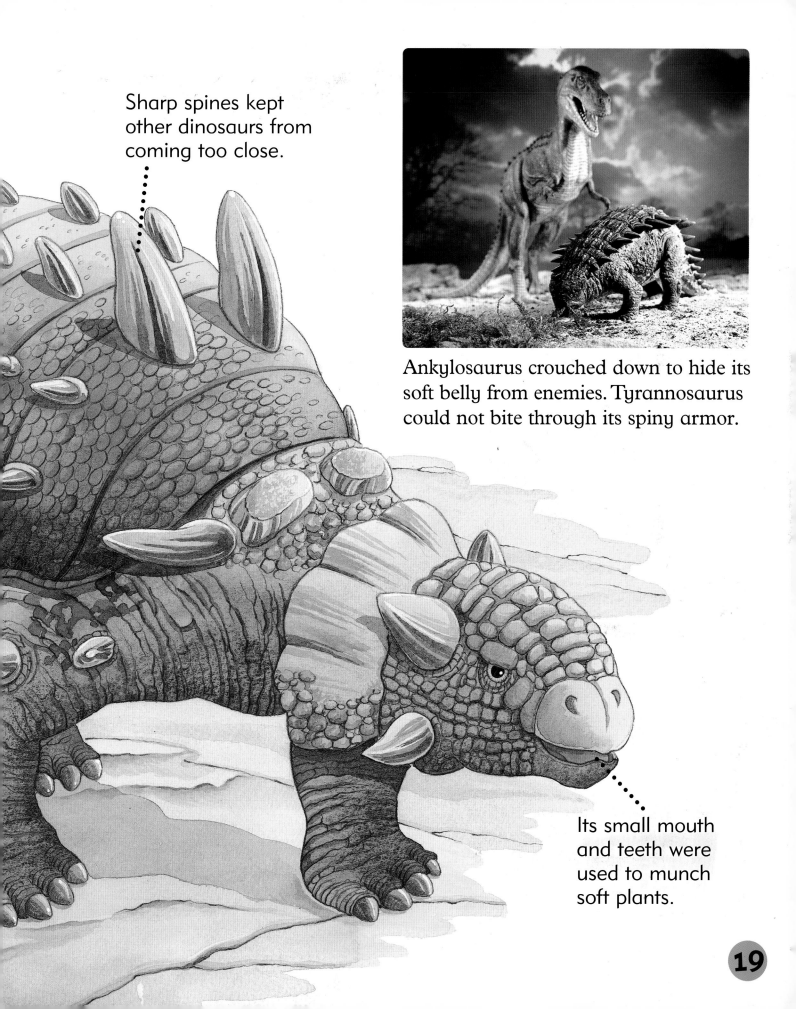

Sharp spines kept other dinosaurs from coming too close.

Ankylosaurus crouched down to hide its soft belly from enemies. Tyrannosaurus could not bite through its spiny armor.

Its small mouth and teeth were used to munch soft plants.

MaiaSaura

Maiasaura had a flattened beak-like snout. Its name means "good mother lizard." Maiasaura laid eggs in a nest, as most other dinosaurs did. But unlike some dinosaurs that left their eggs alone to hatch, Maiasaura guarded her eggs and fed her babies.

It's a fact!

The largest dinosaur egg was almost as big as a soccer ball. Just one of these eggs would be enough to feed 20 people!

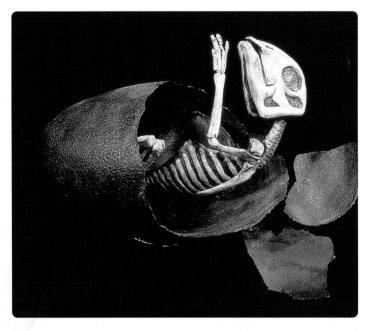

Experts dug up this egg with a baby dinosaur's bones inside. This is how we know that dinosaurs laid eggs.

A mother Maiasaura dug a cozy nest in the sand and laid her eggs inside.

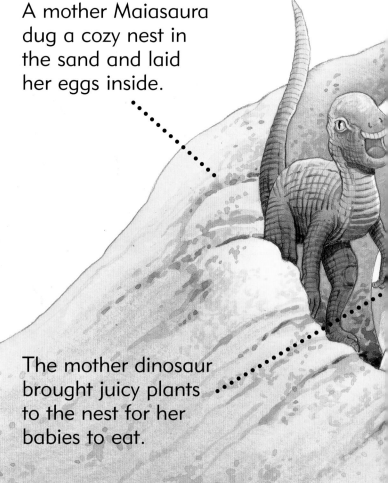

The mother dinosaur brought juicy plants to the nest for her babies to eat.

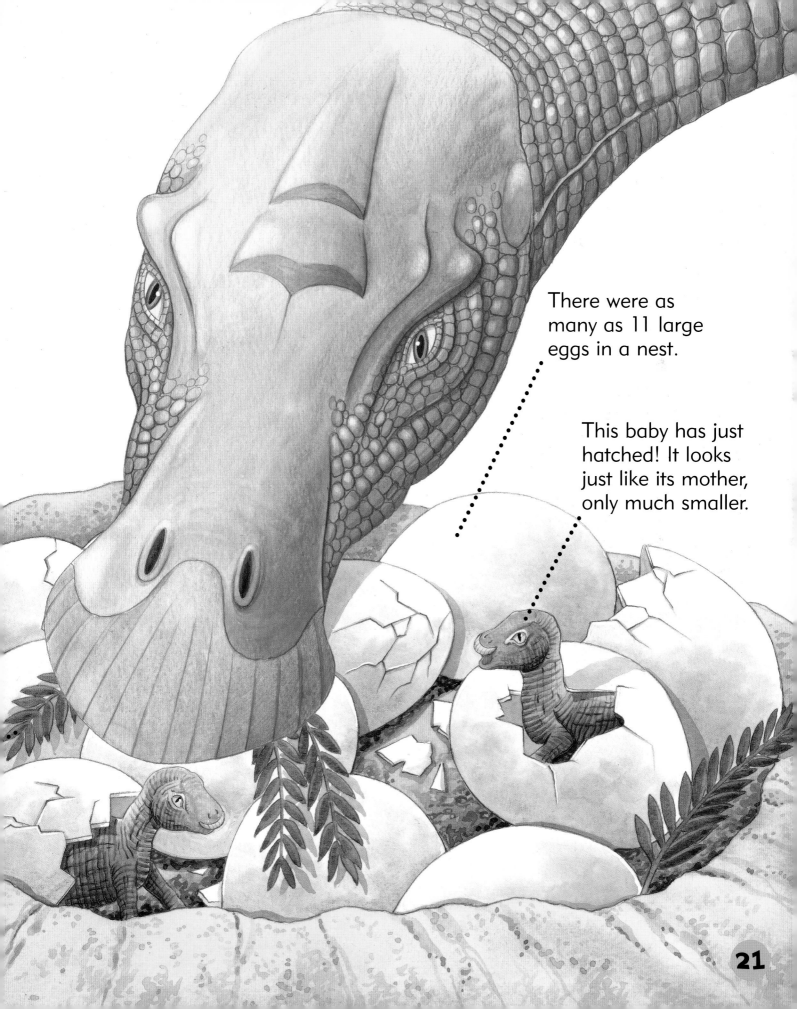

There were as many as 11 large eggs in a nest.

This baby has just hatched! It looks just like its mother, only much smaller.

Velociraptor

Velociraptor was a fast runner and an expert hunter. The small dinosaur probably hunted in a group called a pack. Five or six Velociraptors would team up to catch a larger dinosaur.

A stiff tail helped to keep Velociraptor's body steady.

One of Velociraptor's relatives made this enormous footprint. It has been in this rock for millions of years!

Velociraptor raced along at high speed on its two strong back legs.

Velociraptor's large feet left behind deep footprints in the mud.

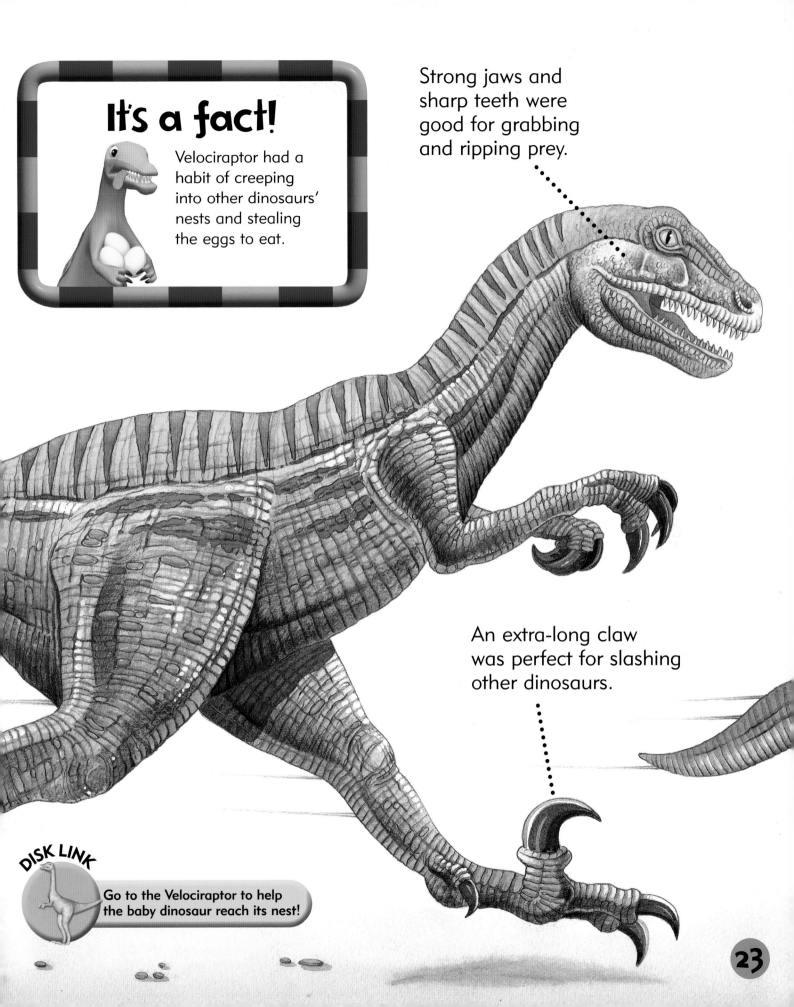

It's a fact!

Velociraptor had a habit of creeping into other dinosaurs' nests and stealing the eggs to eat.

Strong jaws and sharp teeth were good for grabbing and ripping prey.

An extra-long claw was perfect for slashing other dinosaurs.

DISK LINK

Go to the Velociraptor to help the baby dinosaur reach its nest!

Triceratops

Triceratops was one of the last dinosaurs to roam the Earth. These gigantic beasts plodded around, looking for tasty plants to eat. They probably gathered in large groups called herds.

A bony neck frill made Triceratops look scary.

These three pointed horns were useful weapons.

Triceratops sliced up tough leaves and twigs with its sturdy beak.

DISK LINK

Go to the Triceratops to spot dinosaurs out and about.

This skeleton of a Triceratops is in a museum. Can you see the big, bony frill behind its head?

Triceratops had stumpy legs with short, fat toes.

It's a fact!

Dinosaurs died out millions of years ago. A giant rock from space may have hit the Earth, sending up a huge cloud of dust that blocked out the sun. The dinosaurs could not survive.

On the Attack

Tyrannosaurus is about to pounce with its sharp claws and strong jaws. Velociraptor is on the lookout for eggs to eat!

Tyrannosaurus

Maiasaura

Velociraptor

26

Words you know

Here are some words that you learned earlier. Say them out loud, then try to find the things in the picture.

teeth	nest	eggs
frill	horns	toes

Triceratops

Which dinosaur has a bony frill around its head?

An uninvited guest at the party

Major, Minor and Mini Diplodocus had all hatched from their eggs on the same day. They were growing into tall, young dinosaurs with long, stretchy necks. In a few days, it would be their seventh birthday.

"Let's have a birthday picnic," suggested Major Diplodocus, excitedly.

"Great idea!" replied Mini. "We could invite all our friends here to Jurassic Swamp!"

"Just as long as they're vegetarians," warned Minor Diplodocus.

The dinosaurs wrote their invitation list.

"I'm asking the big Diplodocus family next door. They're crazy!" laughed Major.

"And Stegosaurus," said Minor. "We can play Ping-Pong over his plates!"

"Pterodactylus," added Mini, "Brachiosaurus and... Allosaurus."

Everybody went quiet.

"I don't think so," said Minor, "he's NOT a vegetarian. He'll eat you."

"Ooops," squirmed Mini. "Yes, he's got really sharp teeth. I forgot."

The dinosaurs finished making their invitations. Their friend Pterodactylus gathered them in his beak and delivered them by airmail. Then they began preparing the food – a juicy moss salad, crunchy fern sandwiches, and a huge leaf-and-mud birthday cake. They were licking the bowl when Pterodactylus returned.

"All delivered," he said, "and everyone said they could come. One thing, though— I spotted Allosaurus crashing around the forest while I was chatting with Stegosaurus. I hope he didn't hear us."

At last the big day arrived. To be on the safe side, Minor Diplodocus asked Pterodactylus to keep guard overhead. "You never know," he whispered.

"Sure," nodded Pterodactylus. "It's a lovely day for flying. Just make sure you save me some of that mud cake."

29

Major organized the games. First there was a running race. Mini and Minor were neck and neck all the way, but then Major shot into the lead to take the trophy.

"It's not fair!" complained Stegosaurus. "You had a head-and-neck start! My plates and short front legs slowed me down. Let's race again!"

"Forget it!" said all three Diplodocus at once. "You're just a bad loser!"

Next was the wrestling competition. Minor and Mini lost in no time, so it was up to Stegosaurus and Major to fight it out. Thwack! Crunch! Stegosaurus swung his sharp, spiky tail at Major Diplodocus's leathery skin.

"Ouch!" cried Major. "If Ankylosaurus were here, you'd have no chance. *He's* got a big, bony club on his tail."

"Yeah, well, he's *not* here!" grinned Stegosaurus, swinging his tail once more.

"OK! You win!" groaned Major.

It was finally time for the birthday picnic. All the dinosaurs were starving. Soon they were busily munching and scrunching their lunch. Pterodactylus swooped down for his share, then flew back into the air.

"What a feast!" exclaimed Stegosaurus happily. "Eating is my favorite pastime."

"And mine," said Mini with her mouth full of leaves.

The dinosaurs were about to start on the birthday cake when they heard lots of flapping and squawking above their heads.

"Oh, no!" shouted Major. "That's Pterodactylus. He must have spotted—"

"ALLOSAURUS!" gasped Mini. There was a blood-curdling roar from the trees, and the ground started to shake. Allosaurus thundered out of the forest, licking his lips and snapping his jaws. His razor-sharp claws gleamed in the sun.

"He's coming," squawked Pterodactylus. "I've counted his teeth. He's got 70!"

"I don't care how many teeth he's got!" yelled Major Diplodocus. "What do we do?"

"Run?" suggested Pterodactylus.

Allosaurus stormed into the picnic site, stamped on the sandwiches, and stomped through the birthday cake. Then he sniffed the air and slashed at the nearest piece of flesh. His sharp claws grazed Mini's back. Major and Minor bit into Allosaurus's tail, but their flat, blunt teeth had no effect. They were only useful for grinding up plants. There was no escape.

Suddenly, Pterodactylus flew back.

"Your cousins Brachiosaurus and Apatosaurus are here!" he yelled cheerfully.

A herd of giant, long-necked dinosaurs came pounding out of the trees and beat Allosaurus with their massive tails.

"Quick—into the lake!" shouted Major Diplodocus, seeing a chance for escape.

The young dinosaurs ran as fast as they could. Splashing and crashing, they waded deep into the lake. Allosaurus stood panting and raging on the banks, fed up with the chase.

Safe at last, Major, Minor, and Mini caught their breath.

"What's the matter, Allosaurus?" they shouted. "Can't you swim?"

Allosaurus lowered his head and lumbered away, his stomach rumbling.

"We beat him!" the dinosaurs cheered. And three very excited and relieved young dinosaurs splashed in the water as all their friends sang Happy Birthday.

Puzzles and Activities

Now try out these puzzles and activities! You can print out copies from your disk, or make photocopies from the book!

Match It!

Can you match these dinosaurs to their names? Fill in the dotted line from the picture of the Maiasaura to its name. Then match the other dinosaurs to their names. Look back at the dinosaurs in the book if you need help.

Stegosaurus

Maiasaura

Diplodocus

Triceratops

Tyrannosaurus

Dinosaur Days

Lots of dinosaurs are roaming around. Can you spot ten differences between these two pictures? When you find a difference, circle it in picture 2.

1

2

In a Jumble!

Unscramble the letters to name the parts of the dinosaur's body. Write each word in the box below the mixed-up letters. The first one is done for you.

a t i l

t a i l

y e e

____

l a w c

____

t e o

____

Odd One Out

Look at the top row of dinosaurs. They are all exactly the same except for one. Circle the one that doesn't match. Then do the same for the other rows.

Track the Dinos!

Which dinosaur is making which trail? Follow each set of footprints from the swamp with your pencil to find out.

Letter Pairs

Look at the letters on this page. Fill in the dotted line to join the small **h** to the capital **H**. Now match the other small letters with their capital letters.

Missing Words

Match the words at the bottom of the page to the parts of the Stegosaurus in the picture. Write each word in the right box. The first one is done for you.

s p i k e

spike   head   tail   plate

Now match the words to the picture of the Maiasaura.

nest   baby   egg   mother

Egg Trail

Starting at the nest, follow the trail of eggshells with your finger. Each eggshell has a letter on it. As you make your way down the trail, fill in the letters in the spaces at the bottom of the page. What word have you made?

Dinosaur Quiz

Read each question, then check **Yes** or **No** to answer. You can find all the answers in this book. The first one is done for you.

1 Is Compsognathus a small dinosaur?

(Go to page 6.) Yes ✔ No ☐

2 Are dinosaurs still alive today?

(Go to page 25.) Yes ☐ No ☐

3 Can a dinosaur egg be as big as a car?

(Go to page 20.) Yes ☐ No ☐

4 Is Tyrannosaurus taller than you?

(Go to page 17.) Yes ☐ No ☐

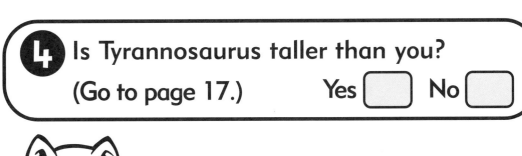

5 Can Allosaurus eat small dinosaurs whole?

(Go to page 8.) Yes ☐ No ☐

Connect the Dots

What's in the picture? Starting with the letter a, connect the dots in alphabetical order. The alphabet is shown below to help you.

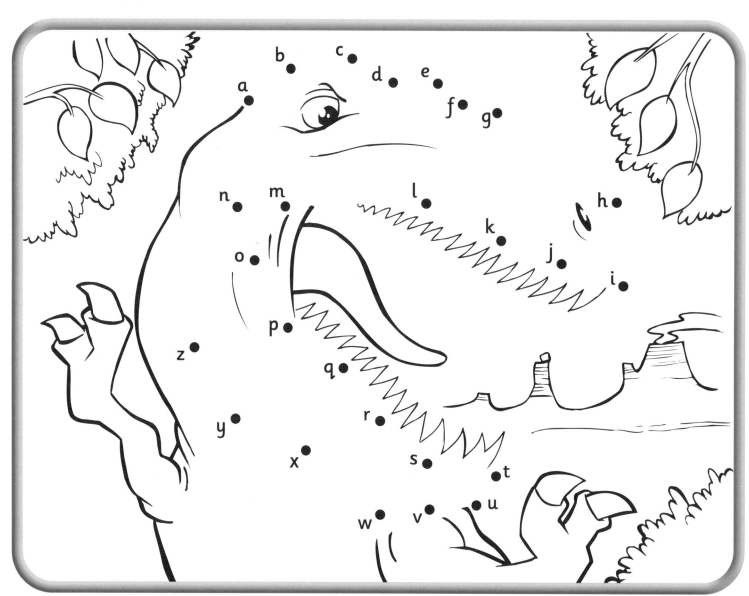

a b c d e f g h i j k l m n o p q r s t u v w x y z

44

Find the Herd!

Help the Stegosaurus find his way through the maze to the rest of his herd. Make sure he doesn't pass any hungry meat-eating dinosaurs on the way!

Dino Word Search

There are six dinosaur words hidden in the grid below. Can you find them? Look across from left to right and from top to bottom. Use the picture clues to help you. The first one is done for you.

teeth

tail

claw

t	h	o	r	n	e	w
a	l	p	t	p	s	c
i	a	e	e	l	t	l
l	n	l	y	a	v	a
b	t	e	e	t	h	w
s	x	a	r	e	d	f
o	m	e	o	n	r	l

plate

horn

eye

Answers

page 34

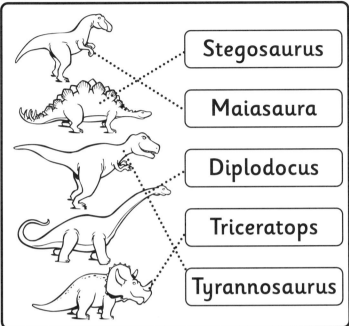

Stegosaurus

Maiasaura

Diplodocus

Triceratops

Tyrannosaurus

page 35

page 36

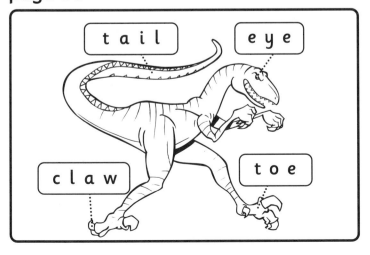

t a i l

e y e

c l a w

t o e

page 37

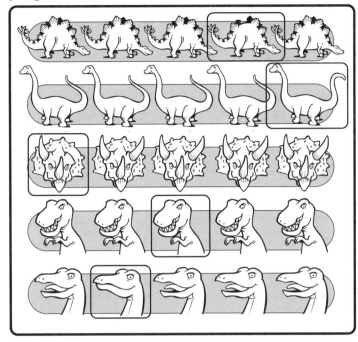

page 38

page 39

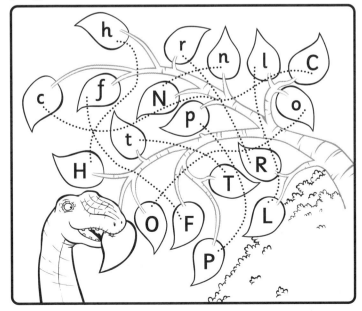

page 40

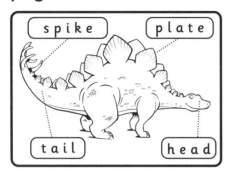

spike | plate
tail | head

page 41

mother
nest
egg | baby

page 42

d i n o s a u r

page 43

1 = yes
2 = no
3 = no
4 = yes
5 = yes

page 44

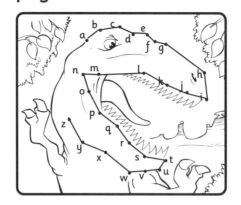

page 45 Below is the quickest route. You may have found others.

page 46

t	h	o	r	n	e	w
a	l	p	t	p	s	c
i	a	e	e	l	t	l
l	n	l	y	a	v	a
b	t	e	e	t	h	w
s	x	a	r	e	d	f
o	m	e	o	n	r	l

Index

To find a dinosaur or one of the ancient animals in the book, look it up in the list below. The numbers show you which pages to look at.